How Nurses Use Math

By Sarah Glasscock

Math Curriculum Consultant: Rhea A. Stewart, M.A.,
Specialist in Mathematics, Science,
and Technology Education

CHELSEA CLUBHOUSE
An Imprint of Chelsea House Publishers

Math in the Real World: How Nurses Use Math

Chelsea Clubhouse
An imprint of Chelsea House Publishers
132 West 31st Street
New York NY 10001

Library of Congress Cataloging-in-Publication Data
Glasscock, Sarah, 1952-
        How nurses use math / by Sarah Glasscock; math curriculum consultant, Rhea A. Stewart.
            p. cm. — (Math in the real world)
        Includes index.
        ISBN 978-1-60413-607-4
        1. Mathematics—Juvenile literature. 2. Nurse—Juvenile literature. I. Title. II. Series.
QA135.6.G58 2009
510—dc22   2009020199

Chelsea Clubhouse books are available at special discounts when purchased in bulk quantities for businesses, associations, institutions, or sales promotions. Please call our Special Sales Department in New York at (212) 967-8800 or (800) 322-8755.

You can find Chelsea Clubhouse on the World Wide Web at http://www.chelseahouse.com

Developed for Chelsea House by RJF Publishing LLC (www.RJFpublishing.com)
Text and cover design by Tammy West/Westgraphix LLC
Illustrations by Spectrum Creative Inc.
Photo research by Edward A. Thomas
Index by Nila Glikin
Cover printed by Yurchak Printing, Landisville, Pa.
Book printed and bound by Yurchak Printing, Landisville, Pa.

Photo Credits: 4: David Buffington/Photodisc/Photolibrary; 6: DreamPictures/Vstock/Blend Images RF/ Photolibrary and iStockphoto; 8: Novastock/Photolibrary; 10: Fancy/Photolibrary; 13: Radius Images/ Photolibrary; 14: Corbis/Photolibrary; 16: PhotoAlto/Odilon Dimier/Getty Images; 18: Michael N. Paras/ age fotostock/Photolibrary; 19: Jose Luis Pelaez Inc/Blend Images RF/Photolibrary; 20: Image Source/ Photolibrary; 22: Barros & Barros/Getty Images; 23: iStockphoto; 24: Paul Shambroom/Photo Researchers, Inc.; 26: JGI/Blend Images RF/Photolibrary.

Printed and bound in the United States of America

This book is printed on acid-free paper.

All links and Web addresses were checked and verified to be correct at the time of publication. Because of the dynamic nature of the Web, some addresses and links may have changed since publication and may no longer be valid.

Table of Contents

Answers and helpful hints for the You Do the Math
activities are in the Answer Key.

Words that are defined in the Glossary are
in **bold** type the first time they appear in the text.

Taking Care of People

Nurses work in many different places. They work in schools, hospitals, and doctors' offices. Some nurses visit people in their homes. Nurses care for people in all of these places. In schools, nurses may give students eye tests. In hospitals, nurses make sure that patients are comfortable. Nurses take their **temperature** and give them medicine.

You have probably seen nurses at work. When you go to the doctor's office, the nurse is often the first person you see.

No matter where they work, nurses do many important tasks. They use math in many of these tasks. Nurses count and measure. They add, subtract, multiply, and divide.

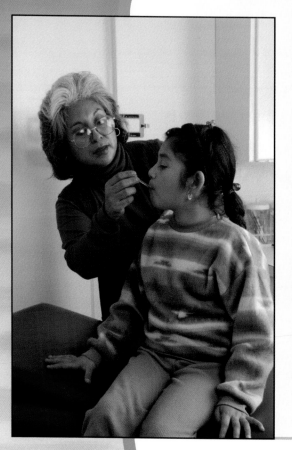

A school nurse takes a student's temperature

Taking Temperature

Nurses use math when they check a

person's **vital signs**. One important vital sign is body temperature. The normal body temperature for a person is about 98.6 degrees Fahrenheit (°F). A high temperature tells a nurse that a person has a fever. When you have a fever, it often means that your body is fighting some sort of **infection** or illness.

A student goes to the school nurse. She says she feels hot. The nurse puts a thermometer into her mouth or ear. A thermometer is a tool that measures temperature. After a few minutes, the nurse takes out the thermometer and reads it. She sees that the student's temperature is 100.8°F. The student's temperature is about 2°F above normal. The nurse says the student has to go home.

You Do the Math

How Is the Temperature?

A person's temperature is the amount of heat that his or her body produces. Look at the information below about low, normal, and high temperatures. The symbol < means "less than." The symbol > means "more than."

Low Temperature	Normal Temperature	High Temperature
< 97.6°F	97.6°F–99.6°F	> 99.6°F

A school nurse takes the temperature of 4 students:

Malia: 99.3°F   **George:** 99.9°F   **Sonja:** 101.2°F   **Sean:** 96.9°F

For each one, decide if the student's temperature is low, normal, or high.

Giving Eye Tests

School nurses give different tests to students. Nurses give hearing tests to find out how well students can hear. They also give vision, or eye, tests to find out how well students can see. To give a vision test, a nurse needs to measure carefully and use **ratios**.

To test vision, the nurse has the student stand exactly 20 feet from an eye chart that is hanging on the wall. Then, she asks the student to read the letters on the chart. (A person who already wears glasses may keep them on during the test.) The letters on the top lines of the chart are large. The letters on the lower lines are smaller. Each line on the chart is smaller than the one above it. The student begins reading at the top

This boy taking an eye test covers his right eye with a tool as he reads the eye chart using his left eye.

and continues reading down until he comes to a line that's too small for him to read.

Measuring Vision

Vision is written as a ratio. Generally, a person is considered to see very well if that person has 20/20 vision. (You say that the person has "twenty-twenty vision.") This means that at a distance of 20 feet from the chart, the person can read the line that most people are expected to be able to read from that distance (but the person cannot read the smaller line below it).

Sometimes an eye test shows that a student needs glasses. The test might show that the student has 20/50 vision. At 20 feet, this student can't read lower than the line that most people are expected to be able to read from 50 feet away.

The nurse will let the student's parents know what the eye test showed. With glasses (or contact lenses), this student may be able to have 20/20 vision.

You Do the Math

Evaluating Vision

To become a pilot in the U.S. Air Force, your vision must be at least as sharp as 20/20 with glasses. Stefan's vision with glasses is 20/30. Can he become a pilot?

Keeping Records

School nurses also keep records. They collect information about students' height, vision, and hearing. They also keep records of any medicines that students are taking and when the medicines should be taken. Keeping these records helps the school and the nurse keep students healthy. The school nurse compares the information for each student collected at different times and studies how it may have changed.

A nurse in a doctor's office prepares to give this boy a vaccination.

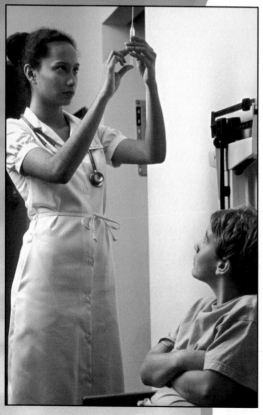

Vaccines

Vaccines are an important item that a school nurse keeps track of. When a person is vaccinated, he is given a substance that will protect him from getting a specific disease. For example, a polio vaccine protects someone from catching the disease polio. Some vaccines contain a combination of substances, so that they protect against more than one disease.

By the time people are 18, they may be vaccinated for as

many as a dozen or more illnesses. Different vaccines are intended to be given at different ages. Some vaccines are given only once. Others have to be given more than once.

Some of the illnesses that vaccines protect against, such as diphtheria, can spread very easily from person to person. These illnesses can be serious, so vaccinating people against them is important.

You Do the Math

Keeping Track of Vaccinations

Doctors recommend that children get different vaccines according to a specific schedule. The table below shows recommendations of the U.S. Centers for Disease Control for when some vaccines for children should be given through age 12.

Recommended Vaccines and Ages	
Vaccine	**Give at Ages**
Diphtheria/tetanus/pertussis	2 months, 4 months, 6 months, 15–18 months, 4–6 years, 11–12 years
Hepatitis B	right after birth, 1–2 months, 6–18 months
Polio	2 months, 4 months, 6–18 months, 4–6 years
Influenza (flu)	every year, starting at the age of 6 months

1. Of the four vaccines in the table, which one is recommended to be given for the first time at the youngest age?

2. If a child's parents and doctor follow the recommendations in the table, by the time the child is 5 months old, which of the four vaccines will the child have received?

Taking the Pulse

A call comes into the hospital. A hiker has fallen in the mountains. He has hurt his leg and cannot walk. An emergency room nurse grabs her medical kit—and her helmet. She jumps into a waiting helicopter behind the pilot. They fly off to pick up the hiker and bring him back to the hospital.

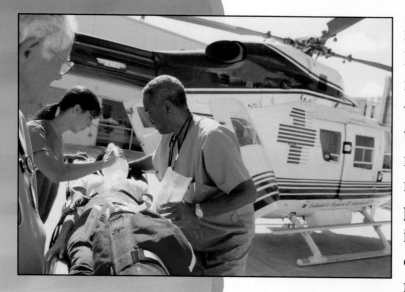

Nurses help an injured patient who has just arrived at the hospital by helicopter.

When the hiker is on board the helicopter, the nurse checks his vital signs. His temperature is normal. Next, the nurse checks his **pulse**. Your pulse is a measurement of your heart rate—the number of times your heart beats in a minute.

The nurse presses two of her fingertips on the hiker's wrist. The wrist is a pulse point. Pulse points are places on the body where you can feel the blood pumping through an artery (a type of blood vessel).

Counting Beats

The nurse counts the number of pulse beats for 15 seconds. She counts 30 beats. The nurse knows that there are 60 seconds in a minute and that 60 = 4 x 15. So she multiplies the number of beats she counted in 15 seconds by 4 to find the number of beats per minutes (bpm):

$$30 \text{ beats} \times 4 = 120 \text{ bpm}$$

The normal pulse rate for an adult is between 60 and 100 bpm. The hiker's pulse rate is higher than normal. He's upset, so his heart may be beating faster than usual.

The nurse checks the hiker's pulse rate 10 minutes later. He is calmer now. His pulse rate is 95 bpm, which is within the normal range (it is between 60 and 100). Soon, the hiker will be at the hospital, where nurses and doctors will care for him.

You Do the Math

Checking Patients

Nurses in hospitals check patients' pulse rates every day. Nurse Rodriguez just checked the three patients in room 304, counting pulse beats for 15 seconds each. She got the following results:

Kevin: 17   **Jeff: 22**   **Philip: 28**

Which of these patients had pulse rates in the normal range of 60 to 100 bpm?

Measuring Medicine

At the hospital, the hiker is taken to the emergency room. Then, he is moved to a room on another floor of the hospital. The hiker stays there for a few days. A different nurse cares for him there.

The nurse reads the hiker's chart. The chart contains the doctor's orders, including what kind of medicine to give and how much of it to give. Orders for medicine are called **prescriptions**. The nurse checks to see if the medicine is in stock. That floor of the hospital doesn't have the medicine the hiker needs. So the nurse must call the hospital **pharmacy**. A hospital pharmacy is a place where medicine and medical supplies are kept.

How Much Medicine?

One of a hospital nurse's most important jobs is to make sure to give the right medicine in the right amount to each patient. When the nurse calls the pharmacy, she makes sure she reads the name of the medicine correctly. She repeats the name, too. She also repeats the strength of the medicine the doctor ordered. The strength tells how much medicine is in each pill or in a certain quantity of liquid. A medicine can come in different strengths, so it is important to get the correct one. The strength of medicine is usually measured in metric units, such as grams (g), milligrams (mg), liters (L), and milliliters (mL).

In this case, the doctor has ordered medicine in the strength of 50 milligram pills. The nurse must make sure that the hiker gets 50 milligrams of medicine. If the hiker got 10 milligrams, the medicine would be too weak to be effective. If he got 100 milligrams, the medicine would be too strong.

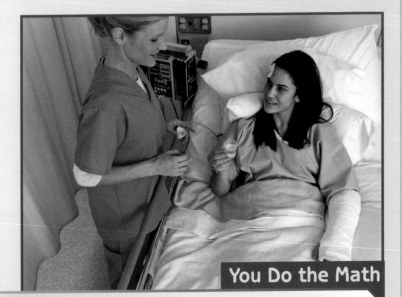

You Do the Math

Figuring Out How Much Medicine to Give

A woman who has broken her arm is in the hospital. The doctor has ordered medicine for her in the strength of 50 milligram pills. The hospital pharmacy has the medicine only in 25 milligram pills. What can the nurse do to make sure the woman receives the correct amount of medicine?

Taking Care of the Tiniest Babies

In another part of the hospital, nurses are taking care of the tiniest babies. These nurses are called **neonatal nurses**. *Neo* means "new." *Natal* means "birth." Neonatal nurses take care of newborn babies.

Most newborn babies are healthy, but some may not be. Some may have been born too early. Most babies are in their mother's **womb** for about 40 weeks before they are born. If a baby is born too early, the baby is said to be **premature**. Doctors say that a baby is premature if it is born before 37 weeks in the womb.

A hospital nurse gives a newborn one of the baby's first meals.

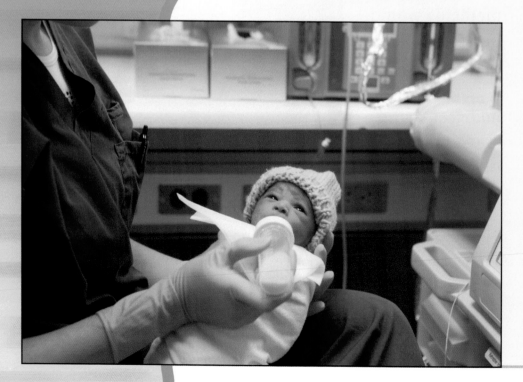

Special Care

Premature babies may need special care. Since they were born earlier than usual, they didn't have as much time to develop. Some premature babies have trouble breathing, so special equipment may be needed to help them breathe. Premature babies also have thin skin and very little body fat. It's harder to keep their tiny bodies warm. Special beds and lights provide heat for them.

Neonatal nurses use special thermometers to check premature babies' temperatures. The thermometer remains on a baby's skin. A sticker keeps it in place.

Neonatal nurses pay careful attention to a premature baby's other vital signs. They attach patches called leads to the baby's chest. These leads count the baby's heartbeats and breaths. The information is shown on a screen. The neonatal nurses read the numbers on the screen. The nurses are checking to see that the number of heartbeats and number of breaths per minute don't go too high or too low.

You Do the Math

Counting the Number of Weeks

Babies are usually born after about 40 weeks in the womb. Premature babies are born after less than 37 weeks. A baby born after 42 weeks is said to be postmature. Suppose a baby is born after 238 days. How many weeks is that? Is the baby premature, postmature, or neither?

15

Working in a Doctor's Office

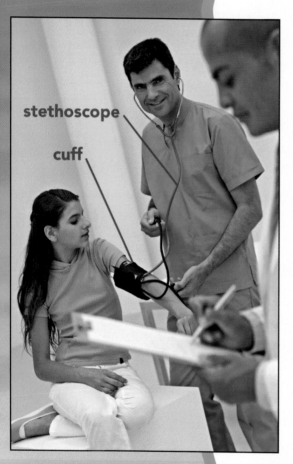

stethoscope

cuff

A patient visiting her doctor gets her blood pressure checked by a nurse.

A new patient arrives at the doctor's office. She has come for a check-up to make sure she is healthy. The woman waits for a few minutes, and then a nurse takes her into a room. Since this is the patient's first visit, the nurse takes her medical history. He asks questions about her health and the health of her family. The nurse listens to the patient. He carefully records all the information on the patient's chart.

The nurse has the patient stand on a scale to check her weight. Then, the nurse checks the patient's vital signs. The nurse checks her **blood pressure**. Blood pressure is the measurement of the force with which blood moves through your arteries as your heart beats. The nurse wraps part of the patient's arm in a special cuff and pumps air into the cuff. He uses a tool called a **stethoscope** to listen to the blood pumping in the pulse point in the patient's arm. Then, he lets the air out of the cuff and listens to the blood pumping in the pulse point again.

Blood Pressure Numbers

Blood pressure is expressed as a ratio between two numbers. The first number is the pressure when the heart beats and pumps blood. The second number is the pressure when the heart is at rest between beats.

The patient's blood pressure is 115/78 (we say this "one hundred fifteen over seventy-eight"). Most doctors think that, for an adult, blood pressure is in a healthy, or normal, range if it is not lower than 90/60 and not higher than 120/80. So the nurse knows this patient's blood pressure is in the normal range. Her first number, 115, is not lower than 90 and not higher than 120. Her second number, 78, is not lower than 60 and not higher than 80.

You Do the Math

Blood Pressure

During his workday in the doctor's office, the nurse also took the blood pressure of five other patients. These were the results:

    150/100   **80/50**   **110/70**   **112/75**   **160/110**

Which of these blood pressures are in the normal range of 90/60 to 120/80?

Refilling Prescriptions

Nurses who work in a doctor's office perform many tasks. One of them may be helping patients with their prescriptions.

Sometimes, a patient calls the doctor's office because he needs a refill of a prescription. The prescription tells what kind of medicine a doctor has ordered for a patient. The prescription also tells the amount the patient should take and how often to take it. When the patient needs a refill, it means he has run out of medicine and needs a new supply.

Making Sure It's Time for a Refill

The nurse looks at the patient's chart. The patient takes 2 pills each day. On the chart, the doctor has written that the medicine can be refilled twice.

A note also says that the medicine has already been refilled once. But is it time for the medicine to be refilled again?

Nurses will often call a pharmacy to order a refill of a patient's medicine.

The nurse sees that the last refill was 7 weeks ago. There are 7 days in a week, so 7 weeks is 49 days (7 × 7 = 49). If the patient takes 2 pills each day, he's taken 98 pills in those 49 days (49 × 2 = 98). The medicine comes in a bottle of 100 pills. Since the patient has taken 98 pills, it is time to refill the medicine.

The nurse calls the pharmacy to order the refill. She is sure to give the name and strength of the medicine correctly. Now the patient can go to the pharmacy to get his medicine.

A mother picks up medicine for her daughter at the pharmacy.

You Do the Math

When Should Daria Get Her Medicine?

Some medicines are taken only once a day. Other medicines are taken more often. Daria has a sore throat. For a few days her mother must give her medicine 3 times a day and always the same number of hours apart. If Daria gets her first dose at 7 A.M., when should her mother give her the second dose? When should her mother give her the third dose? (Remember: There are 24 hours in a day.)

Nurse Practitioners

A **nurse practitioner** (sometimes called an NP) is a special type of nurse who has gone to school longer than other nurses. A nurse practitioners can examine patients, order special tests, and make a **diagnosis**. Making a diagnosis means that the NP identifies what illness a patient has. The NP then decides how to treat it. Nurse practitioners can also prescribe medicine. (Usually it is a doctor who prescribes medicine, and most types of nurses do not.)

Helping a Sick Baby

A father brings his baby to the NP's office. The baby is 5 months old and seems sick. The nurse practitioner

A nurse practitioner examines a young patient in her office.

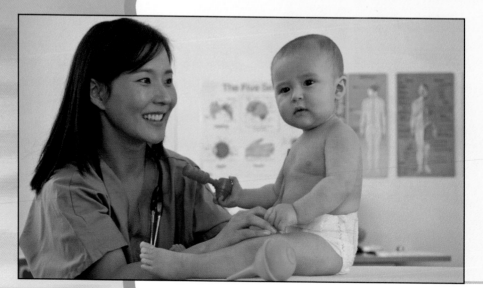

takes the baby's temperature. It's high: 101.5°F. She asks the father some questions: Has the baby been eating? Has the baby been crying more than usual? Has the baby been sleeping more or less than usual?

The baby has not been eating or sleeping well. He has been crying a lot. The nurse practitioner thinks she knows what's wrong with the baby. She orders some tests to confirm her diagnosis. She needs to be sure.

The results of the tests come back quickly. The nurse practitioner was right. The baby has an infection. The NP prescribes medicine. A few days later, the baby is feeling better.

You Do the Math

Calculating the Right Dose

Often, the amount of medicine a child should take is lower than the amount that's right for an adult. Sometimes, a nurse practitioner has to do math to calculate the proper amount of medicine for a child. The nurse practitioner can use a formula to figure out the right dose. First, divide the child's weight by 150. Then, multiply the result by the adult dose. Here's an example. A child weighs 30 pounds. The adult dose is 30 milligrams. To calculate the child's dose:

$$30 \div 150 = \frac{1}{5}$$

$$\frac{1}{5} \times 30 = 6$$

The child's dose is 6 milligrams.

Maria is a 9-year-old girl. She weighs 60 pounds. The nurse practitioner wants to prescribe medicine for her. The medicine has an adult dose of 20 milligrams each day. What dose should the NP prescribe for Maria?

Visiting Nurses

Some nurses visit patients in their homes. These nurses are called visiting nurses. In one day, a visiting nurse may see a 6-month-old baby and a 106-year-old man. No matter who the patient is, the nurse usually begins the visit by checking the person's vital signs.

Visiting a Baby

A nurse visits the home of a 6-month-old baby. She measures the baby's length. Then, she weighs the baby using a special scale. Comparing the length and weight to a growth chart, the nurse sees that the baby's growth is normal.

Next, the nurse checks the baby's **respiratory rate**. Respiratory rate is another vital sign. It is the number of breaths taken in a minute. Sometimes, when the patient is a baby, the nurse checks respiratory rate by watching the baby's chest rise and fall. The nurse counts the number

A visiting nurse sits a baby on a special scale to check the child's weight.

of breaths he takes in 30 seconds. There are 60 seconds in a minute, and 30 × 2 = 60. If the nurse multiplies the number of breaths the baby took in 30 seconds by 2, the product will be the number of breaths he took in a minute—his respiratory rate. The nurse sees that the baby is breathing well.

Before leaving, the nurse asks the baby's parents if they have any questions. She does not leave until she has answered all of them.

Your respiratory rate will go up if you run during a soccer game or while playing another sport.

You Do the Math

What Is Your Respiratory Rate?

Respiratory rate is the number of breaths a person takes in a minute. The rate increases when you exercise. Count the number of breaths you take in 30 seconds. Multiply by 2 to find your respiratory rate. (Remember: There are 60 seconds in a minute.) Then do 25 jumping jacks and figure out your respiratory rate again. How has it changed?

Taking Care of Older Patients

A visiting nurse visits an older woman. She talks to the woman and checks her vital signs. She checks the woman's blood pressure, and she checks her respiratory rate using a stethoscope. Before placing the stethoscope on the woman's chest, the nurse warms it between her hands. Then, the nurse listens through the stethoscope and counts the number of breaths the woman takes in 30 seconds. She takes 12 breaths in 30 seconds. The nurse multiplies by 2 to get the

A nurse checks vital signs while visiting one of her patients.

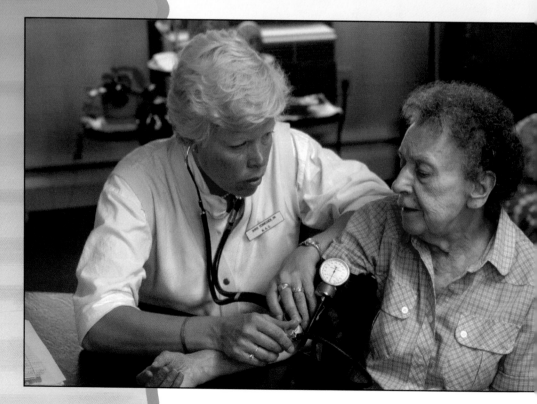

number of breaths the woman takes in a minute: $12 \times 2 = 24$.

The woman's respiratory rate is 24 breaths per minute. Many doctors think that the normal respiratory rate for an adult is about 15 to 20 breaths per minute. So, the patient's respiratory rate is a little high, but the nurse isn't surprised. She knows that the woman has a medical condition that makes it harder for her to breathe. She sometimes needs oxygen to help her breathe more easily. She gets the oxygen from an oxygen tank. A tube goes from the oxygen tank to her nose.

Checking Equipment

One of the visiting nurse's jobs is to check the patient's oxygen tank. She makes sure oxygen is flowing freely through the tank and into the nose tube. She also makes sure the correct amount of oxygen is flowing through the tube. If it isn't, the nurse turns a knob on the oxygen tank to change the rate at which the oxygen flows.

You Do the Math

Calculating Respiratory Rate

Many doctors think that the respiratory rate for a healthy adult should be about 15 to 20 breaths per minute. This is sometimes called the normal range. If a woman takes 8 breaths every 30 seconds, what is her respiratory rate for 1 minute? (Remember: There are 60 seconds in 1 minute.) Is her respiratory rate in the normal range?

Expecting a Baby

A visiting nurse visits a woman who is going to have a baby soon. The baby is in the mother's womb. The nurse listens to the baby's heartbeat using a special type of stethoscope. The baby's heart sounds healthy. It's beating at a rate of about 150 beats per minute. That's much faster than a child's heart or an adult's heart usually beats, but it's a healthy rate for a baby that's due to be born in about 3 weeks. The nurse checks the mother's vital signs, and they are all fine.

Gaining Enough Weight

Finally, the nurse checks the mother's weight. The mother is 8 months pregnant. Since she became pregnant, she has gained 25 pounds. The nurse says that's a healthy amount of weight for her to gain to help her baby grow.

A woman who is going to have a baby needs to eat more foods that are healthful, to help her baby grow.

Counting Calories

A woman who is going to have a baby needs to add more **calories** from healthful foods to her diet. The extra calories help her baby grow and develop. In the first 3 months of pregnancy, she needs to add about 150 calories a day to her diet. The table below shows the number of calories found in different foods. Which of the five lists of items below can the woman add to her daily diet in order to take in about 150 additional calories but not much more than that?

List 1: yogurt, broccoli
List 2: sweet potato, vegetable soup
List 3: egg, apple

List 4: broccoli, cheddar cheese
List 5: peanut butter, banana

Number of Calories in Different Foods	
Food	**Calories**
milk (8 ounces)	136
broccoli (1 cup)	30
oatmeal (1 bowl)	93
cereal (1 bowl)	110
egg (1 large)	74
apple (1 medium)	72
sweet potato (1 medium)	115
cheddar cheese (1 ounce)	114
vegetable soup (1 bowl)	122
spaghetti (2 ounces)	211
tuna (2 ounces)	66
peanut butter (1 tablespoon)	96
cod (6 ounces)	140
peas (1 cup)	67
banana (1 medium)	105
bagel (1 medium)	195
orange juice (8 ounces)	112
yogurt (4 ounces)	119

If You Want to Be a Nurse

In this book, you've read about nurses who work in schools, hospitals, doctors' offices, and people's homes. You may be interested in becoming a nurse yourself!

To become a nurse, you must first graduate from high school. Then you must attend nursing school for 1 to 4 years, depending on the kind of nurse you want to be. After nursing school, you must pass a special exam. Passing the exam shows that you are ready to work as a nurse.

Nurses must care about people and be good at communicating with them. They must be careful about details and be able to stay calm in emergencies. They need good math skills. To see what being a nurse is like, some high school students volunteer to work in their local hospital.

You can also study subjects in school that will help you develop the skills that nurses need. Make sure to take English, science, and math classes. Nurses need to be good at adding, subtracting, multiplying, and dividing.

Answer Key

Pages 4-5: Taking Care of People:
Malia's temperature is normal. George's temperature is high. Sonja's temperature is high. Sean's temperature is low.

Pages 6-7: Giving Eye Tests:
No, Stefan cannot become an Air Force pilot. With 20/30 vision, he can see at 20 feet away what many people can see from 30 feet away. His vision is not as sharp as that of someone who has 20/20 vision.

Pages 8-9: Keeping Records:
1. Hepatitis B vaccine: right after birth. 2. Diphtheria/tetanus/pertussis, hepatitis B, and polio. Influenza vaccine is not recommended until a child is 6 months old.

Pages 10-11: Taking the Pulse:
Kevin and Jeff have pulse rates in the normal range. Kevin's pulse rate is: 17 (in 15 seconds) x 4 = 68 bpm. Jeff's pulse rate is 22 x 4 = 88 bpm. Philip's pulse rate is 28 x 4 = 112 bpm, which is outside the normal range of 60 to 100.

Pages 12-13: Measuring Medicine:
The nurse can give the patient 2 of the 25-milligram pills. The nurse can add or multiply to calculate this. 25 milligrams + 25 milligrams = 50 milligrams, or 25 milligrams x 2 = 50 milligrams.

Pages 14-15: Taking Care of the Tiniest Babies:
34 weeks. There are 7 days in a week, so to find the number of weeks in 238 days, divide 238 by 7. $238 \div 7 = 34$. The baby is premature.

Pages 16-17: Working in a Doctor's Office:
110/70 and 112/75 are in the normal range. 150/100 is higher. 80/50 is lower. 160/110 is higher.

Pages 18-19: Refilling Prescriptions:
First, divide the number of hours in a day (24) by 3 to figure out the number of hours between Daria's doses. $24 \div 3 = 8$. If Daria took her first dose at 7 A.M., she should take her second dose at 3 P.M., which is 8 hours after 7 A.M. She should take her third dose at 11 P.M., which is 8 hours after 3 P.M.

Pages 20-21: Nurse Practitioners:
Maria should take 8 milligrams. $60 \div 150 = \frac{2}{5}$. $\frac{2}{5} \times 20 = 8$.

Pages 22-23: Visiting Nurses:
Here's a possible answer: Say you count 11 breaths in 30 seconds. $11 \times 2 = 22$ breaths per minute, which is your respiratory rate. After you do 25 jumping jacks, you count 17 breaths in 30 seconds. $17 \times 2 = 34$. Your respiratory rate has increased, which happens after exercise.

Pages 24-25: Taking Care of Older Patients:
Her respiratory rate is 16 breaths per minute. Multiply the number of breaths in 30 seconds by 2 to get the number of breaths in 60 seconds, or 1 minute. $8 \times 2 = 16$. The respiratory rate is in the normal range. It is not less than 15, and it is not more than 20.

Pages 26-27: Expecting a Baby:
Adding the foods in list 1 or list 3 or list 4 would add almost 150 calories to the woman's daily diet: 1. yogurt and broccoli: $119 + 30 = 149$. 3. egg and apple: $74 + 72 = 146$. 4. broccoli and cheddar cheese: $30 + 114 = 144$. Adding the foods in list 2 or list 5 would add more than 200 calories to the woman's daily diet: 2. sweet potato and vegetable soup: $115 + 122 = 237$. 5. peanut butter and banana: $96 + 105 = 201$.

Glossary

blood pressure—The measurement of the force with which blood moves through the arteries as the heart beats and pumps blood through the body.

calorie—A unit for the amount of energy supplied by a food item.

diagnosis—The identification of an illness from its signs and symptoms.

infection—An illness that is caused by germs that enter the body and that often can be spread from one person to another.

neonatal nurse—A nurse who takes care of newborn babies.

nurse practitioner—A nurse who has advanced training and can perform some of the tasks of doctors, such as examining a patient and making a **diagnosis**.

pharmacy—A place in a hospital where medicines and medical supplies are kept and given out. A store or a part of a store where medicines are sold.

premature—Happening or arriving before the usual time; said of a baby who is born after fewer than 37 weeks in the **womb**.

prescription—A written order for a medicine, telling the kind, strength, amount to take, and how often.

pulse—A measurement of heart rate, or the number of times the heart beats per minute.

ratio—A comparison of two numbers.

respiratory rate—The number of breaths taken in one minute.

stethoscope—An instrument used to listen to sounds in the human body, including breathing and heartbeats.

temperature—The level of heat in the human body.

vaccine—A substance that protects a person against a specific illness.

vital signs—Signs that show life in a person; the vital signs are **temperature**, **pulse** (or heart rate), **blood pressure**, and **respiratory rate**.

womb—The part of a woman's body where a baby grows and develops before being born.

To Learn More

Read these books:

Cunningham, Kevin. *Nurse*. Ann Arbor, Mich.: Cherry Lake, 2009.

Schwarz, Eloise. *Nurses Are Patient People*. Bloomington, Ind.: AuthorHouse, 2006.

Thompson, Lisa. *Trauma Shift: Have You Got What It Takes to Be an ER Nurse?* Minneapolis, Minn.: Compass Point Books, 2009.

Trumbauer, Lisa. *What Does a Nurse Do?* Berkeley Heights, N.J.: Enslow Publishers, 2006.

Look up these Web sites:

Kids into Nursing
http://www.unmc.edu/nursing/careers/Default.htm

LifeWorks: Explore Health and Medical Science Careers
http://www.science.education.nih.gov/LifeWorks.nsf/feature/index.htm

U.S. Government Career Voyages: Health Care—Nursing
http://www.careervoyages.gov/healthcare-nursing.cfm

Key Internet search terms:

healthcare, nurse, nursing

Index

About the Author

Sarah Glasscock has written fiction and nonfiction books for adults and children.

RICHMOND HEIGHTS